COUNCIL *on*
FOREIGN
RELATIONS

Council Special Report No. 94
June 2022

The Case for a New U.S.-Saudi Strategic Compact

Steven A. Cook and Martin S. Indyk

The Council on Foreign Relations (CFR) is an independent, nonpartisan membership organization, think tank, and publisher dedicated to being a resource for its members, government officials, business executives, journalists, educators and students, civic and religious leaders, and other interested citizens in order to help them better understand the world and the foreign policy choices facing the United States and other countries. Founded in 1921, CFR carries out its mission by maintaining a diverse membership, with special programs to promote interest and develop expertise in the next generation of foreign policy leaders; convening meetings at its headquarters in New York and in Washington, DC, and other cities where senior government officials, members of Congress, global leaders, and prominent thinkers come together with Council members to discuss and debate major international issues; supporting a Studies Program that fosters independent research, enabling CFR scholars to produce articles, reports, and books and hold roundtables that analyze foreign policy issues and make concrete policy recommendations; publishing *Foreign Affairs*, the preeminent journal on international affairs and U.S. foreign policy; sponsoring Independent Task Forces that produce reports with both findings and policy prescriptions on the most important foreign policy topics; and providing up-to-date information and analysis about world events and American foreign policy on its website, CFR.org.

The Council on Foreign Relations takes no institutional positions on policy issues and has no affiliation with the U.S. government. All views expressed in its publications and on its website are the sole responsibility of the author or authors.

Council Special Reports (CSRs) are concise policy briefs, produced to provide a rapid response to a developing crisis or contribute to the public's understanding of current policy dilemmas. CSRs are written by individual authors—who may be CFR fellows or acknowledged experts from outside the institution—in consultation with an advisory committee, and are intended to take sixty days from inception to publication. The committee serves as a sounding board and provides feedback on a draft report. It usually meets twice—once before a draft is written and once again when there is a draft for review; however, advisory committee members, unlike Task Force members, are not asked to sign off on the report or to otherwise endorse it. Once published, CSRs are posted on CFR.org.

For further information about CFR or this Special Report, please write to the Council on Foreign Relations, 58 East 68th Street, New York, NY 10065, or call the Communications office at 212.434.9888. Visit our website, CFR.org.

To submit a letter in response to a Council Special Report for publication on our website, CFR.org, you may send an email to publications@cfr.org. Alternatively, letters may be mailed to us at: Publications Department, Council on Foreign Relations, 58 East 68th Street, New York, NY 10065. Letters should include the writer's name, postal address, and daytime phone number. Letters may be edited for length and clarity, and may be published online. Please do not send attachments. All letters become the property of the Council on Foreign Relations and will not be returned. We regret that, owing to the volume of correspondence, we cannot respond to every letter.

This report is printed on paper that is FSC® Chain-of-Custody Certified by a printer who is certified by BM TRADA North America Inc.

CONTENTS

FOREWORD

The United States and Saudi Arabia have maintained a close, if uneasy, relationship for some three-quarters of a century, since President Franklin D. Roosevelt and King Abdulaziz Al Saud established ties aboard the USS *Quincy*. The United States sought to secure a steady supply of oil; Riyadh looked to Washington for security. Mutual antipathy toward communism throughout the Cold War brought the two countries closer together. At the same time, vastly different political systems and values, and diverging views of Israel, made the partnership at times awkward, even strained. In the end, though, strategic considerations prevailed.

In recent years, however, this partnership has become increasingly distant, even estranged. The United States has become sharply critical of human rights abuses within Saudi Arabia, above all the murder of journalist Jamal Khashoggi, along with what Washington viewed as Riyadh's ill-advised war of choice in Yemen. Saudi Arabia, for its part, grew frustrated by what it viewed as U.S. softness on Iran and a decline in American reliability. President Joe Biden, who as a candidate vowed to make Saudi Arabia a "pariah," had refused to speak with its de facto leader, Crown Prince Mohammed bin Salman during his first year in office. The kingdom, in return, has rejected Biden's calls to increase oil production in the wake of Russia's invasion of Ukraine.

Now, however, circumstances may be developing for a reconciliation between the two countries. Russia's war in Ukraine, combined with inflation at home, have contributed to a steep rise in energy prices, thus renewing attention on Saudi Arabia as one of the world's top oil producers, and the only one to have a significant capacity to increase production quickly. At the same time, Iran is edging closer to putting into place the prerequisites of a nuclear weapons program, raising alarms in both Washington and Riyadh. The Biden administration also has an interest in shepherding a normalization of ties between Saudi Arabia and Israel, a development that could assist in managing Iran as well as unlocking progress on the Israeli-Palestinian issue.

In this Council Special Report, Eni Enrico Mattei Senior Fellow for Middle East and Africa Studies Steven A. Cook and Distinguished Fellow Martin S. Indyk call on both countries to recognize their overlapping interests and renovate their relationship, advocating for what they term a new strategic compact. At the heart of their proposed modernization of the original U.S.-Saudi compact would be an agreement to counter the threat from Iran. Using that as the foundation, the U.S. and Saudi governments would need to negotiate a package of reciprocal steps whereby each would make parallel commitments to each other.

Cook and Indyk put forward some basic elements of any such package. To address Saudi Arabia's perception of U.S. unreliability, they argue the United States would need to provide security assurances. Saudi Arabia, for its part, would make a more formal open-ended commitment to stabilize oil prices at reasonable levels. It would also need to wind down its war in Yemen and take further steps to normalize relations with Israel. Finally, Crown Prince Mohammad bin Salman would be required to commit to meaningful political and social reform in addition to taking responsibility for Khashoggi's murder and bringing all directly responsible to justice.

Cook and Indyk argue plainly that "the United States needs a responsible Saudi partner and Saudi Arabia needs a reliable U.S. one." But there should be no illusions that such an ambitious rethinking of the U.S.-Saudi Arabia relationship would be easy to negotiate much less sustain given the two countries' starkly different political systems and their disagreements. The authors, however, make the case that it is worth seeking as such a tie would be far preferable to either a divorce or a narrow reconciliation that failed to address core concerns and differences. This timely Council Special Report provides both historical context and thought-provoking ideas for the future of the U.S.-Saudi relationship.

Richard Haass
President
Council on Foreign Relations
June 2022

ACKNOWLEDGMENTS

We would like to thank the members of the CFR Advisory Committee on the Case for a New U.S.-Saudi Strategic Compact for their time and input. We, alone, are responsible for the content of this Council Special Report. We would also like to thank CFR's president, Richard Haass; James M. Lindsay, the director of studies; Patricia Dorff, editorial director; Cassandra Jensen, associate editor; Christian Kreznar, staff editor; our research associates, Basia Rosenbaum and Francesca Eremeeva, as well as our interns, Olivia Babski, Andrea Kemmerle, Simone Lipkind, and Jordan Rothschild for the time and attention they devoted to this report.

Steven A. Cook and Martin S. Indyk

Acknowledgments

INTRODUCTION

The encounter between President Franklin D. Roosevelt and King Abdulaziz Al Saud aboard the USS *Quincy* in the Suez Canal on February 14, 1945, represents the launching point for relations between the United States and Saudi Arabia. From the start, it was an unlikely partnership. A democratically elected patrician president from a storied American family laid the foundations for a pact with a Bedouin sheikh who ruled a desert kingdom and drew his legitimacy from a puritanical preacher. The deal that developed over time was straightforward. The United States needed unimpeded access to the vast reservoirs of oil beneath Al Saud's desert sands, and Saudi Arabia needed protection from avaricious neighbors and great powers.[1]

Throughout the ensuing years, that pact held despite significant differences between the Western world's leading democracy and the Muslim world's leading autocracy. In recent times, however, a structural shift has emerged. The United States no longer needs as much Saudi oil, and Saudi Arabia has a new, young leader who does not respect the implicit rules of the partnership. This combination is shaking the foundations of the relationship and clouding its future. As the price of oil spiked at $125 per barrel after Russia's invasion of Ukraine in February 2022, Saudi Arabia's crown prince, Mohammed bin Salman, rebuffed President Joe Biden's request that Saudi Arabia play its traditional role of releasing more oil onto the market to tamp down prices, even refusing to take the president's call. To be sure his message was understood in Washington, he began talks with the Chinese about denominating Saudi oil sales to China in yuan rather than dollars.[2]

However, recent developments in the oil market are combining with the United States' retrenchment from the Middle East to produce a paradox: even as American dependence on Saudi oil has dramatically declined and the United States has downgraded the importance of the Middle East in its foreign policy priorities, Saudi Arabia has become more, not less, important. The United States needs to stabilize a volatile region even as the country focuses elsewhere and to moderate oil prices in a market influenced by geopolitics. At the same time, Saudi Arabia's security environment has deteriorated because of a growing threat from Iran, and it has few reliable alternatives to an American security umbrella.

Seventy-seven years after the original Roosevelt-Abdulaziz pact, the changing circumstances require a reassessment of the relationship's value to each side, for if urgent action is not taken, the process of separation that is already under way is likely to accelerate, damaging the interests of both sides. The war in Ukraine has created both the necessity and possibility of taking that remedial action. It would be relatively straightforward to put differences aside and renew the original compact, but given the structural problems in the relationship, that would hardly be sustainable. Sooner rather than later, the problems would return. More basic adjustments are necessary: the United States would need to recognize that during the decades-long transition away from fossil fuels, Saudi Arabia's role in stabilizing oil prices will remain critical; Saudi Arabia would need to recognize that American support for its security will require greater respect for American interests and values. In addition, Saudi Arabia would have to play a more effective and responsible role in promoting stability, regional security, and the resolution of conflicts, and the United States would have to provide backing for that role with stronger and more tangible security assurances.

In short, a fundamental renovation of the basic bargain that has lasted more or less for eight decades is required. This will not be easily achieved; both sides will have to swallow their pride and adjust their policies in essential ways if they are to forge a new strategic compact for the twenty-first century.

ORIGINS

Since the end of World War II, the U.S.-Saudi relationship has been built upon the cornerstones of Saudi Arabian oil and American security guarantees. Energy was the most important component of those ties, but it became intertwined with global concerns, particularly containing the Soviet Union during the Cold War. Although Saudi Arabia had little else to contribute to the global conflict between the United States and the Soviet Union aside from its vast oil reserves and the money they generated, its role would prove indispensable. The Saudi leadership was fiercely anti-communist, and its oil became critical in the reconstruction of Europe after World War II and in the success of the Western-dominated global economic order.

The security-for-oil compact at the heart of the U.S.-Saudi relationship was not without significant challenges. During the October 1973 Arab-Israeli War (also known as the Yom Kippur War), Saudi Arabia led an Arab oil boycott of the United States and its European and Japanese allies to generate Western pressure on Israel to withdraw from Arab territories it occupied after the 1967 Six-Day War. The embargo and the accompanying decision of Middle Eastern oil producers to double the price of their oil generated a recession in the West and long fuel lines in the United States. Relations deteriorated so badly that President Richard M. Nixon's advisors even discussed a military intervention to seize Saudi Arabia's oil fields. Although the Saudis would never again use oil as a weapon in the Arab-Israeli conflict, the 1973 embargo left a lasting impression on a generation of Americans who experienced economic hardship as a result of Saudi Arabia's effort to punish the United States for its assistance to Israel.

The U.S.-Saudi relationship changed dramatically in 1979. In November of that year, the shah of Iran was overthrown, and some sixty-six U.S. diplomats and their Marine Corps guards were taken hostage in Tehran. That same month, extremists laid siege to the Grand Mosque in Mecca. Then, on Christmas Eve 1979, the Soviet Union invaded Afghanistan.

The Iranian Revolution was a huge setback for the United States and posed a threat to Saudi security, but it was also an opportunity for Riyadh. Although Saudi Arabia was one of the United States' "twin pillars" on which it based its strategy for ensuring stability in the Persian Gulf, in reality, U.S. officials looked to Iran to provide regional security and stability. The shah's overthrow and the establishment of the revolutionary Islamic Republic suddenly rendered Saudi Arabia more important to the United States.

Not long after the Americans were taken hostage in Tehran, Saudi militants took over the Grand Mosque in Mecca, driving home for the House of Saud that threats to its stability were not only to be found across the Gulf.[3] The Saudi royal family responded to the challenge to its religious legitimacy by turning to its Wahhabi clerical allies for support. In exchange for their backing against these homegrown extremists, Saudi Arabia's religious establishment was given a free hand to propagate its fundamentalist version of Sunni Islam abroad. This sparked a competition with Iranian efforts to export its revolutionary doctrines to Shiite communities, especially in the Arab world. The ensuing sectarian rivalry would have a devastating effect on Muslim societies around the world, as well as significant and harmful ramifications for U.S.-Saudi relations in the decades to come.[4]

For a moment, however, the U.S.-Saudi relationship benefited dramatically from another event that occurred during those last tense months of 1979—Moscow's military takeover in Afghanistan. From their newly acquired control of Kabul, the Soviets could potentially mount a drive into Pakistan and establish a base of operations adjacent to the Gulf of Oman, through which a significant portion of global oil supply flowed. In response, President Jimmy Carter explicitly committed the United States to defend the oil fields of the Gulf from external aggression, a statement of policy that would come to be known as the Carter Doctrine.[5]

The Soviet invasion generated a decade-long, ultimately successful U.S.-Saudi effort to bleed the Soviets in Afghanistan. The Saudi intelligence services and the CIA played a central role, together with Pakistan's Inter-Services Intelligence agency, in arming and training the anti-Soviet forces, eventually known as the mujahideen. Among these groups, the Saudis worked with a contingent of Arab fighters, led by Osama bin Laden, who became the linchpin of their efforts to supply weaponry and money to the Afghans fighting the Soviets.

Washington and Riyadh also had a common interest in weakening the newly established Islamic Republic of Iran. After Saddam Hussein launched a war on Iran in 1980, Saudi Arabia persuaded the Ronald Reagan administration to tilt in favor of Iraq. The United States provided Saddam with weaponry, military advice, battlefield intelligence, and diplomatic support, and even turned a blind eye when he used chemical weapons against the Iraqi Kurds. Meanwhile, the Saudis and other wealthy Arab Gulf states supplied Saddam with $30 billion to $40 billion of loans to finance Baghdad's war effort.[6]

The U.S.-Saudi partnership suffered a setback in the mid-1980s, when the United States sold weaponry to Iran to secure the release of Americans held hostage in Lebanon by Iran's allies there. In turn, the United States used the proceeds of the sales to fund anti-communist guerillas in Nicaragua, which Congress had prohibited. When the plot became public in 1986, the Saudis were shocked that the United States would assist the Iranian war effort behind their backs.

The disillusionment did not last long. On August 2, 1990, Saddam invaded Kuwait. The deployment of Iraqi troops to the Saudi-Kuwaiti border put Saddam in a position to control the oil supplies of two of the world's most important producers and thereby force up the price. The Saudis were compelled to turn to the United States for protection. In response, President George H.W. Bush deployed an expeditionary force of more than 500,000 troops, complemented by military forces from 36 other countries. The purpose was to protect Saudi Arabia and ensure the free flow of oil at reasonable prices. The subsequent expulsion of the Iraqi army from Kuwait gave full expression to the "oil for security" bargain.

It is ironic that such close and successful cooperation within a decade could generate deep disillusionment on both sides. This outcome was not evident at first. The Gulf War had opened an opportunity for Middle East peace and for the United States and Saudi Arabia to work together on a more positive endeavor. Saudi Arabia facilitated the diplomatic efforts of Secretary of State James Baker to bring the Arab parties to the 1991 Madrid Peace Conference with Israel. The Saudis also appreciated President Bill Clinton's attempts to resolve the Israeli-Palestinian conflict. Justice for the Palestinians had long been a concern for Saudi kings, just as U.S. support for Israel had been a source of tension between them from the beginning of their relationship.[7] Ultimately, however, Crown Prince Abdullah—who became de facto ruler of Saudi Arabia in 1995—was frustrated by Clinton's inability to forge a final peace between the Israelis and Palestinians; Clinton, in turn, was disappointed by the lack of Saudi support for his efforts.[8]

Clinton also pursued a policy of "dual containment" to keep Iran and Iraq—Saudi Arabia's regional adversaries—in check.[9] This required maintaining a robust U.S. military presence inside Saudi Arabia, which provided a target for Iranian and jihadi forces. In late 1995, two bombs outside a Saudi Arabian National Guard facility in Riyadh killed five Americans. Then, in June 1996, Iranian agents operating in Saudi Arabia's Eastern Province bombed an apartment complex in Khobar that housed U.S. military personnel. The attack killed nineteen Americans and raised questions about the complicity of Saudis because the housing complex was supposed to have been well guarded. To make matters worse, Minister of Interior Prince Nayef bin Abdulaziz—who was known for his anti-U.S. sentiments—only grudgingly and episodically cooperated with the U.S. investigation. In time, as the unpopularity of the U.S. military presence in the kingdom became clear, the United States moved its military operations from King Abdulaziz Air Base to a more secluded location southeast of Riyadh and then eventually out of the country altogether.

Intense cooperation during the 1990s only managed to generate disappointment and disillusionment between the United States and Saudi Arabia. Those tensions in the relationship were exacerbated in George W. Bush's presidency by the outbreak of the second Palestinian intifada in 2000. Television broadcasts of Palestinian casualties incensed the Saudis. They also believed that the Bush White House gave the Israelis a "green light" for their iron-fisted strategy in response to the uprising. As a result, Crown Prince Abdullah threatened to reassess bilateral relations with the United States. The crisis in relations was averted when Bush promised the crown prince he would publicly support the establishment of a Palestinian state, which he did in June 2002. Nevertheless, a once robust relationship had grown fragile.

U.S. POLICY SINCE 9/11

The al-Qaeda terrorist attacks on New York and Washington on September 11, 2001, marked a watershed in relations because fifteen of the nineteen men who hijacked the four airliners were Saudi nationals. Osama bin Laden, the mastermind of the plot, was also a scion of one of Saudi Arabia's more important families.[10] Before the 9/11 attacks, 56 percent of Americans had a favorable view of Saudi Arabia; in their aftermath, approval dropped to 27 percent.[11] Nevertheless, the relationship between governments remained cooperative. The Saudis supported the U.S. invasion of Afghanistan, especially after trying and failing to convince the Taliban leadership to hand over bin Laden, who was sheltering there. Still, not until 2003, when al-Qaeda launched a wave of attacks inside Saudi Arabia, did the leadership in Riyadh begin to take the threat of extremism more seriously. Subsequently, U.S.-Saudi counterterrorism cooperation was significantly enhanced.

However, Bush's invasion of Iraq in March 2003 aggravated relations at the official level. The Saudis regarded Saddam as a menace, but as long as Washington remained resolute about containing him, they were not overly concerned. From Riyadh's perspective, even in his weakened state under international sanctions, Saddam still functioned as a necessary counterweight to Tehran. The Saudi leadership was also skeptical of Bush's declared objective of a more open, democratic, and vibrant Iraqi society—an unwanted contrast to Saudi Arabia in the unlikely event such a policy proved successful. Its greater fear was that regime change would produce chaos, providing an opportunity for the Iranians to deepen their influence in Iraq via the Shiite majority there.

Although Iraq's much diminished capacity to resist Iran was the result of U.S. hubris and poor planning, the Saudis saw something else. They suspected that Washington, by engineering Tehran's newfound position of influence in Baghdad, actually sought a rapprochement that would make Iran the United States' primary partner in the Gulf again.

In the fall of 2003, Bush announced to great fanfare in Washington—and consternation in Riyadh—that he would be pursuing a "forward strategy of freedom" in the Middle East. The Saudis listened in horror as Secretary of State Condoleezza Rice declared in Cairo in June 2005 that for six decades the United States had pursued stability at the expense of democracy in the Middle East and had achieved neither. Now, she said, "we are taking a different course. We are supporting the democratic aspirations of all people."[12]

Although the Bush administration focused its efforts on political reform in Egypt and the Palestinian Authority, the Saudis feared that they would be subjected to the same treatment and its destabilizing effects across the region. The kingdom had come to depend on the United States to promote stability in its dangerous neighborhood; now Washington seemed determined to subvert this goal.

When President Barack Obama took office in 2009, Saudi Arabia's worst nightmares were fulfilled. Initially, the Saudis were pleased that the new president appointed a special envoy for Israeli-Palestinian peace, brought pressure to bear on the Israeli government over settlement construction, and pressed Israel's Prime Minister Benjamin Netanyahu to support the establishment of a Palestinian state. They also welcomed Obama's outreach to Muslims in his speech at Cairo University in June 2009 and were relieved that the new president de-emphasized promoting democracy in the region.

At the same time, the Obama administration's determination to reach out to Iran and to withdraw from Iraq—leaving the country in the hands of a new Shiite leadership, including a prime minister who was clearly beholden to Tehran and others who were openly supported by the Iranians—were causes for deep concern in Riyadh. Anxiety turned to alarm when the Obama administration openly supported the Arab uprisings (often called the Arab Spring) and Obama himself called on Egyptian President Hosni Mubarak to step down in the face of widespread protests. If the United States could so easily turn on its closest ally in the Arab world, the Saudi royals feared what could happen to them. Yet, in the case of the Syrian uprising, the United States chose not to intervene after Bashar al-Assad militarized his response to protests with significant assistance from Iran. By 2012, three Arab capitals—Baghdad, Beirut, and Damascus— were under Iranian sway. From the Saudi perspective, U.S. policy was directly responsible for Tehran's increased influence in two of

them. This concern was compounded by Obama's resolve to negoti-
ate a nuclear accord with Iran, coupled with his intention to reorient
U.S. foreign policy by "pivoting" to Asia. The Saudis wondered what
would become of the U.S. commitment to their security if the United
States were to turn its back on the region, all the while facilitating
Iran's efforts to fill the vacuum.

JASTA AND JCPOA

During the Obama administration's nuclear negotiations with Iran,
Congress passed the Justice Against Sponsors of Terrorism Act
(JASTA), which amended several laws, weakening claims of "sovereign
immunity" that foreign governments could invoke to shield themselves
in U.S. courts. This legislation was intended to open the way for victims
of the 9/11 attacks and their families to sue Saudi Arabia on the claim of
official Saudi complicity with al-Qaeda. Obama vetoed the bill, but the
Senate overrode it by a vote of ninety-seven to one despite Saudi Arabia's all-out lobbying campaign against the bill. To add insult to injury,
Obama implied to the *Atlantic*'s Jeffrey Goldberg that Saudi Arabia's
greatest security threat was internal and suggested that the Saudis
needed to "share" their neighborhood with the Iranians.[13]

The White House had its own frustrations with the Saudis, including their willingness to bankroll counterrevolutionaries in the region
and their opposition to the nuclear agreement with Iran known as
the Joint Comprehensive Plan of Action (JCPOA). The administration appeared unsympathetic to Saudi concerns that the agreement
did nothing to address Iran's subversive regional activities. Partly in
response, in March 2015, Saudi Arabia and the United Arab Emirates
(UAE) intervened militarily in Yemen to reverse the Iranian-backed
Houthi forces' takeover of the capital, Sanaa. They expected a quick
victory. To reassure Saudi Arabia at a time when the JCPOA was being
finalized, the Obama administration agreed to provide refueling, intelligence, and arms support for the Yemen war. However, as the war
dragged on and civilian casualties mounted from indiscriminate Saudi
bombing, Obama reversed course and suspended the transfer of weapons to Saudi Arabia.[14]

The tensions were in plain view when Obama traveled to Saudi
Arabia in the spring of 2016. In an unmistakable snub, the king chose not
to greet the president on arrival in the kingdom, sending the governor of
Riyadh instead. Saudi Arabia's leaders now looked toward an incoming
Donald Trump administration with hopes of a change of course.

They were not disappointed. Shortly after Trump was sworn into office, he chose Riyadh as the site of his first foreign visit; confirmed a large sale of weaponry negotiated by the Obama administration (pressing the Saudis to purchase more); signaled his intention to withdraw from the JCPOA and apply "maximum pressure" to Iran; and resumed arms supplies for Saudi Arabia's war in Yemen. Trump also initially gave the go-ahead for the Saudi, Egyptian, and Emirati blockade of Qatar, though quickly reversed course and took a more evenhanded approach when he came to understand that Qatar hosted and paid for the largest U.S. base in the region. After Saudi officials murdered Jamal Khashoggi and dismembered his body at the Saudi Arabian consulate in Istanbul, Trump shielded Crown Prince Mohammed bin Salman—whom the CIA believed to be directly responsible—from accountability.

During Trump's tenure, issues that would previously have caused a crisis in U.S.-Saudi relations drew only muted responses from Saudi officials. Notable among these was the president's decision to recognize Jerusalem as Israel's capital and move the U.S. embassy from Tel Aviv to Jerusalem, and his subsequent vision for Middle East peace, which offered Israel support for further dispossession of the Palestinians. King Salman did, in time, convene an Arab summit to denounce the embassy move. However, when Bahrain and the UAE signed normalization agreements with Israel under the auspices of the Trump administration, abandoning the Saudi Arab Peace Initiative that linked normalization to the prior settlement of the Palestinian issue, the Saudis signaled their acquiescence. They immediately opened an air corridor for commercial airlines flying between Tel Aviv and Dubai and Manama across Saudi Arabia. At the same time, Riyadh reaffirmed its support for the establishment of a Palestinian state with East Jerusalem as its capital.

Overall, the Trump administration presided over a period of warm and cooperative relations between the royal court and the White House, but underneath the comity, serious differences were still steadily eroding the relationship's foundations. First, congressional Democrats and Republicans (though more of the former than the latter) became increasingly critical of the U.S. role in Saudi Arabia's Yemen intervention, opposed the Qatar blockade, sought to ban arms sales, decried the jailing of the crown prince's critics, and condemned the murder of Khashoggi.

When a September 2019 Iranian drone and missile attack on the Abqaiq and Khurais oil facilities in Saudi Arabia temporarily cut off

50 percent of Saudi Arabia's oil production, Trump's unwillingness to respond threw into doubt the basic understanding at the center of the bilateral relationship. Then, in January 2020, the United States killed Qasem Soleimani, the head of Iran's Islamic Revolutionary Guard Corps. The Saudi press celebrated Soleimani's demise, but the official reaction was far more circumspect, counseling caution and de-escalation in fear that Iran would retaliate on Saudi Arabian soil and Trump again would leave them to their own devices.[15]

Those episodes could be dismissed as examples of Trump's incoherent approach to foreign policy, but they also indicated a shift in U.S. priorities. After two decades of wars in the Middle East, the American people had grown weary of the huge investment in the region, which seemed only to produce negative returns. At the same time, China's rise presented a new and more complex threat to U.S. interests, requiring policymakers to shift focus from the Middle East to Asia. That process of retrenchment began under Obama but was enhanced under Trump, with his isolationist instincts. Biden reinforced the trend, operationalizing his mantra "America is back" by ending the foreign entanglements that have undermined American power and prestige. This was clearly manifested in Biden's determination to withdraw all U.S. forces from Afghanistan, but the United States' shambolic retreat underscored the message for the Saudi leadership: the Middle East had become a lower priority for Washington than at any time in the previous two decades, and the United States had become a less reliable security partner as a result.

Further eroding the basic bargain was the natural gas revolution and the dramatic increase in shale oil production in the United States, which rendered Middle Eastern oil and the defense of Saudi Arabia less important in the minds of American policymakers. The United States has become the world's largest oil and natural gas producer, well ahead of Russia and Saudi Arabia. In the process, the United States has gone from importing almost 1,000,000 barrels per day (bpd) of crude oil from the Persian Gulf in 2001 to only 250,000 bpd in 2020, which represents a mere 12 percent of U.S. oil imports.[16]

Climate change has added impetus to this dynamic by increasing the pressure on the U.S. government to reduce dependence on fossil fuels for the United States' energy future. With automobile manufacturers shifting to electric vehicle production and the oil majors shifting investment into alternative, sustainable sources of energy, dependence on Saudi oil will lessen over time, notwithstanding the temporary increase in demand because of Russia's war in Ukraine.

On the Saudi side, the rise to power of Mohammed bin Salman, the king's son, has also shaken the relationship's foundations. MBS, as he has come to be known, represents a new generation of Saudis who seek a more modern, outward-looking country. The crown prince has dispensed with the cautious and consensus-building approach of his father and uncles in favor of an aggressive and interventionist style of rule.

Bin Salman pursued several policies that earned him plaudits in the United States and Saudi Arabia—especially among the younger generation—for his commitment to modernization. These included allowing Saudi women the right to drive, restricting the morals police, reigning in clerics, and curtailing government support for the export of Wahhabi fundamentalist ideology.

Yet, as he accumulated power and authority, bin Salman's autocratic tendencies have become an increasing problem for Washington. He sidelined all rivals, including Mohammed bin Nayef—the designated crown prince and a favorite of the U.S. intelligence community for his counterterrorism cooperation. He arrested some five hundred business leaders and princes in what bin Salman said was a crackdown on corruption but was also a shakedown and part of a broader effort to consolidate his power through intimidation. He also forced the resignation of the Lebanese prime minister, launched the ill-fated military intervention in Yemen, imposed the blockade of fellow Gulf Cooperation Council (GCC) member Qatar, reportedly sought to destabilize King Abdullah II of Jordan, and ordered the murder of Jamal Khashoggi. In March 2022, in one day, he ordered the execution of eighty-one people. The combination of those actions undermined the goodwill the crown prince had gained among Americans and many of their elected leaders for his modernizing ambitions.[17]

A TIME TO REASSESS

During his election campaign, Biden labeled bin Salman "a thug" and promised to treat the Saudis "as the pariahs that they are." Once in the Oval Office, he called the crown prince's father and warned of the need for a "recalibration" of the relationship. He ended U.S. support for bin Salman's war in Yemen and paused all offensive arms sales to the kingdom. He ordered the release of an intelligence assessment of the Khashoggi murder, which concluded that the crown prince had "approved" the assassination. Although he stopped short of sanctioning the crown prince, he made it clear he would not deal with him, designating Secretary of Defense Lloyd Austin as his interlocutor and signaling that the de facto ruler of Saudi Arabia was not welcome in Washington. One of the first communications between Austin and bin Salman was to inform him that the United States was withdrawing Patriot and Terminal High Altitude Area Defense (THAAD) anti-missile batteries from the kingdom.[18] At the time, Saudi airports and oil facilities were undergoing sustained Houthi missile and drone attacks. These withdrawals, together with the drawdown of U.S. forces in the Gulf and the Biden administration's negotiations with Iran over a nuclear deal, sent an unmistakable signal to Saudi Arabia of U.S. unreliability. Each side felt the other was no longer willing to observe its commitments to the relationship.

Given Biden's rhetorical commitment to putting values back into U.S. foreign policy, he cannot easily live with bin Salman's behavior. By the same token, the personal offense that bin Salman now feels, combined with his perception that Saudi Arabia can no longer rely upon the United States to come to its defense, is leading him to adopt a hedging strategy involving closer relations with China and Russia, the United States' adversaries. If both sides fail to change the current trajectory, the United States and Saudi Arabia are likely to drift even further apart. Saudi Arabia no longer believes it can rely on Washington for its security, and the United States no longer believes it can rely on Riyadh to stabilize the oil market.

The challenge for American and Saudi policymakers at this nadir in the relationship, then, is to step back and reassess what would prove most worthwhile: going their separate ways, resuscitating the old compact, or attempting to create a new, more reliable understanding.

IT'S STILL OIL, STUPID

The reassessment necessarily begins with oil. Even though U.S. dependence on Middle Eastern oil has now dropped dramatically and is unlikely to increase anytime soon, Saudi Arabia today possesses 17 percent of the world's proven oil reserves and provides 11 percent of world oil production.[19] Major U.S. trading partners in Asia still depend heavily on Saudi crude oil imports (see figure 1). Interruption to the free flow of oil from Saudi Arabia will, therefore, still harm the global economy and Middle Eastern stability for the foreseeable future.

Saudi Arabia also remains the only "swing producer" in the oil market because it is the only oil-producing country with an excess capacity of one to two million bpd. It is therefore able to influence the price of oil in a way that can help or harm the United States and

Figure 1. CRUDE OIL IMPORTS FROM SAUDI ARABIA (2020)

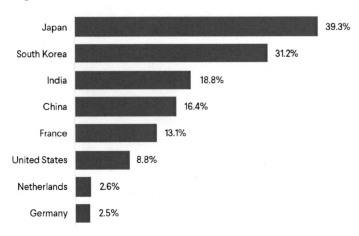

Source: Observatory of Economic Complexity.

The Case for a New U.S.-Saudi Strategic Compact

the global economy. This reality was driven home in 2020 when Saudi Arabia flooded the market with its oil in a dispute with Russia over pricing, driving the price to zero at the start of the COVID-19 pandemic and dealing a blow to the U.S. shale oil industry in the process (although it was a boon to American consumers and oil-consuming industries). Then, as the world's economies rebounded from the pandemic, demand for oil picked up unexpectedly and many producers had difficulty increasing their exports, driving up the price of oil dramatically. As the price approached $100 a barrel, fueling fears of growing inflation, Biden dispatched envoys to Saudi Arabia to request that the kingdom release some of its spare capacity to tamp down the price. The crown prince demurred. Then, with Biden facing a crisis with Russia over Ukraine that threatened to disrupt Europe's energy supplies and drive the price of oil even higher, the president again sent diplomats to Riyadh to persuade bin Salman to open the spigot. With American pleas falling on deaf ears, the renewed importance of Saudi Arabia to U.S. interests was driven home quite starkly.

This is not a temporary aberration that will fade once things settle down in Europe. Notwithstanding American and European efforts to switch from fossil fuels to sustainable energy sources, the transition is moving slowly, though the U.S. intelligence community expects it to gain speed after 2030.[20] Economic growth is likely to increase demand for fossil fuels over the next two decades because alternative energy sources will not close the gap in time. European determination, prompted by Vladimir Putin's aggression in Ukraine, to end dependence on Russian oil and gas will increase its dependence on Middle Eastern sources. Meanwhile, global investment in oil and gas production is declining to record lows as corporations are pressed to shift their investments to clean energy. This is particularly true of the oil majors, which are curtailing oil production and now produce only 15 percent of the world's oil supplies. Their production will be replaced by state-controlled oil and gas companies. Indeed, Qatar, Saudi Arabia, and the UAE are all investing large sums to increase production capacity to take advantage of this increase in demand while it lasts. Saudi Arabia has announced plans to invest $50 billion to increase its production by some 700,000 bpd by 2027.[21] Qatar intends to double its gas production in the next three years. That, in turn, makes the Persian Gulf more, not less, important to the United States. As policy experts Meghan O'Sullivan and Jason Bordoff point out, "[They] are best positioned to be the last producers standing . . . giving them outsize influence until demand falls to much lower levels"—and that is not expected to happen for another three decades.[22]

As long as the industries of Europe and Asia are dependent on Gulf oil, there is the ever-present danger of Iranian efforts to disrupt Gulf oil supplies. In short, the free flow of oil and gas from the Gulf at reasonable prices has returned as a priority for U.S. interests.

MUSLIM WORLD LEADERSHIP

The Saudi king's custodianship of the two holy mosques of Mecca and Medina makes his country the leading Muslim nation. What happens in Saudi Arabia will have a ripple effect in the Arab and Muslim worlds. Saudi Arabia's export of its puritanical Wahhabist form of Sunni Islam has been detrimental to many Muslim societies across the globe. Its sectarian rivalry with Iran has helped to fuel conflicts that have devastated Lebanon, Syria, and Yemen. Bin Salman's decision to curtail these radicalizing activities at home and abroad in favor of promoting a more moderate and tolerant Islam is a welcome development that could resonate in other Muslim countries. Should that effort falter at home, however, extremist Islam could come roaring back, creating a ripple effect across the Islamic world. That threat underscores the importance that successful Saudi modernization still has in a broader conception of U.S. strategic interests. The United States therefore maintains an interest in the kingdom's social and political stability and economic progress.

The same is true for the crown prince's ambitious modernization agenda. His Vision 2030 plan seeks a total transformation of the Saudi economy designed to wean it off its heavy dependence on oil. This more diversified approach to economic development requires investing in downstream production, expanding the private sector, developing a new tourism sector, building huge infrastructure projects, attracting foreign direct investment, increasing female participation in the workforce, and cutting unemployment by half (from 12 percent to 7 percent). If successful, this modernization effort could do much to head off an economic crisis as oil revenues decline over time.

Five years into implementation, however, Vision 2030 is falling far short of its employment, private-sector, and foreign-investment goals and has been further impeded by the COVID-19 pandemic. The crown prince has countered those setbacks by mobilizing the Saudi private sector and its public investment fund to invest $3.2 trillion over the next decade in growing the private sector. However, as the *Economist* points out, this is "a risky bet," potentially flooding the Saudi economy with investment funds and emptying the nation's sovereign wealth fund "to buy a herd of white elephants."[23]

That could end up disappointing the expectations and aspirations of Saudis younger than thirty, who make up more than two-thirds of the population. Bin Salman's relaxing of social strictures, his granting of greater rights to women, and his promotion of public entertainment have satisfied many of them for the time being. If the economic reforms fail to sustain meaningful employment for this generation, however—and they are already falling short—it could generate a significant popular backlash against the king-in-waiting.

AMERICAN RETRENCHMENT

The U.S. interest in a moderate and stable Saudi Arabia also grows as the United States retrenches from the Middle East and refocuses on Asia. Were the United States to leave an unstable vacuum, U.S. policymakers are conscious of the way they could get sucked back into addressing, rather than turning their backs on, the region's problems. For the foreseeable future, the major threat to Middle Eastern stability comes from Iran, a revolutionary state with hegemonic regional ambitions and nuclear weapons aspirations. Since its revolution in 1979, Iran has systematically sought to exploit sectarian divisions, local conflicts, and weak governing institutions across the Arab world to build its influence. As the United States turns to more pressing priorities in Asia and Europe, it needs to help put in place a security framework in this third strategic arena that relies on its regional allies and partners to fill the vacuum. Ironically, in this context, Saudi Arabia's strategic importance to the United States increases, especially because the United States' other Arab allies cannot easily substitute for Saudi Arabia's weight in the regional balance of power. Jordan and the UAE can play important security roles, but they are too small to have a significant effect on the overall balance of power. Egypt is much larger and more capable, but it is preoccupied with its immediate neighborhood and only recently appears willing to play a more assertive, though still cautious, role in countering Iran.[24]

Israel is the other major regional power allied to the United States that can help fill the vacuum. Israel and Saudi Arabia have historically had a common interest in promoting regional stability. In the 1960s, they cooperated covertly in Yemen to counter the destabilizing challenge from Egyptian President Gamal Abdel Nasser. Today, they each perceive Iran as an existential threat to their vital interests. Were it possible to forge a more open strategic collaboration between Israel and Saudi Arabia, the two could together broaden and deepen an Arab-Israeli partnership that is already taking shape because of the common perception by Israel and the Sunni Arab states that Iran is threatening them. With Saudi Arabia involved, this "Abraham Accords Axis" would stretch from the Gulf to the Red Sea and the eastern Mediterranean, encompassing the GCC states, Egypt, Israel, Jordan, Morocco, and Sudan.[25] As strategic cooperation grows, it could provide a robust platform for promoting regional stability that would enable the United States to shift from a dominating role in the regional balance to a supportive one.

Bin Salman has encouraged the development of Saudi Arabia's relations with Israel, albeit out of public view and mostly confined to security issues. The Palestinian issue, however, has come between them. The old-guard Saudi leadership never wavered in its rhetorical support for the Arab cause against Israel and, in particular, in its demand for justice and statehood for the Palestinians. Conscious of the importance the Saudi public placed on establishing a Palestinian state and the destabilizing potential of getting too close to Israel, the Saudi kings preferred to keep their distance, encouraging U.S. endeavors from the sidelines. Given their sensitivity to any threat to social cohesion, they were determined to be the "last to make peace with Israel," as the late King Abdullah declared.

True to character, bin Salman was willing to play a more active role. He partnered with Jared Kushner, Trump's son-in-law and special peace envoy, in trying to foist a pro-Israel deal on the Palestinians.[26] He also green-lighted Trump's decision to move the U.S. embassy to Jerusalem. However, that decision crossed a redline for his father, King Salman, who, as the custodian of the two holy mosques, was not willing to accept Israeli sovereignty over the third holy mosque in Jerusalem. When the UAE decided to normalize relations with Israel, bin Salman approved Bahrain's decision to follow suit and opened Saudi Arabia's skies to direct flights from Tel Aviv to Manama, Dubai, and Abu Dhabi. Those moves helped provide critical momentum to the Abraham Accords. However, absent progress on the Palestinian issue, bin Salman's father was not willing to have Saudi Arabia go the last mile to full normalization.[27]

Nevertheless, the Abraham Accords have created a framework for the burgeoning of security cooperation between Israel and the Sunni Arab states that have signed up. Israel has announced formal security agreements with Bahrain and Morocco. The Israel Defense Forces (IDF) has placed an officer at Fifth Fleet headquarters in Manama, across the Gulf from Iran, and the UAE and Israel are cooperating on missile defense due to attacks on Abu Dhabi by the Iranian-backed Houthis. In short, a strategic architecture in which Saudi Arabia and Israel increase their cooperation with like-minded Arab states to counter Iran's destabilizing regional activism can do much to fill the void created by the U.S. retrenchment from the region.

The problem with the United States' growing strategic dependence on Saudi Arabia, however, is that more often than not bin Salman's forays abroad have undermined the effort to contain Iran. His blockade of Qatar, for example, split the GCC and made the Qataris more dependent on Tehran because they were left with no choice but to use Iranian airspace for their vital lines of communication.

The most damage, however, has been caused by bin Salman's intervention in the Yemeni civil war, which has helped generate the worst humanitarian crisis in the world today.[28] The unintended but foreseeable consequence has been to increase Iran's influence on Saudi Arabia's southern flank, as the Houthis—who control almost all of northern Yemen, including Sanaa, the capital—turned to the Iranian Revolutionary Guard Corps for weapons, missiles, drones, and training. The war has spilled over into Saudi Arabia's southern provinces, and the Houthis are also targeting Saudi airfields and oil facilities as far north as Riyadh and Jeddah. In its seventh year, the war has become a high-cost, no-gain quagmire for Saudi Arabia and a low-cost, high-gain opportunity for Iran.

Bin Salman has belatedly realized that Saudi Arabia's interests lie in ending the war he should have never started. That, however, is now much easier said than done. The Houthis, with Iran's support, are intent on consolidating their grip on the northern half of the country. Although willing to engage in tactical truces, particularly if they help consolidate their rule, they will have little interest in a negotiation that would do anything other than legitimize their victory.[29] They have no reason to share power in Sanaa. The Saudis, by contrast, are now under heavy pressure to end the war and do not have the means to force the Houthis to the negotiating table. Like the United States in Vietnam and Afghanistan, Saudi Arabia is faced with the choice of a forever war or an ignominious withdrawal with no assurance that it will end Houthi attacks on Saudi Arabia. Increasingly desperate, bin Salman has turned to Iran in the hope that it will restrain its Houthi proxies.[30] Should the Iranians be willing to try, however, the price will be a consolidation of their influence on the Arabian Peninsula, one of the things that bin Salman sought to prevent by intervening in Yemen in the first place.

At a minimum, then, the United States needs a Saudi leadership that is more conscious of its role in promoting a stable regional equilibrium and more sensitive to the way its actions can upset that equilibrium. Whether bin Salman will play that more responsible role is unclear. His facilitation of a truce in Yemen is a positive indicator. However, growing U.S. dependence on increased Saudi oil production seems only to have convinced bin Salman that he has no need to change his behavior. As he told the *Atlantic* in March 2022, the potential in the world today is in Saudi Arabia, "and if you want to miss it, I believe other people in the East are going to be super happy."[31] If bin Salman comes to believe that he now has sufficient leverage to force the Biden administration to accept him as he is, he may have little incentive to act more responsibly.

On the other hand, bin Salman has no reason to adopt this more reliable role when he sees the United States reducing its involvement in the region in a way that raises questions about the U.S. commitment to Saudi security. Saudi Arabia therefore needs a U.S. leadership that it, too, can rely on to support the kingdom's fundamental security. At a time when the United States is focused on serious challenges to its interests in Asia and Europe, that is a tall ask, even if the White House were inhabited by a president willing to overlook bin Salman's human rights abuses at home or rash engagements abroad.

THE SHORTCOMINGS
OF CURRENT OPTIONS

If each side simply stays on its current course, the future of U.S.-Saudi relations is bleak. Left to its own devices, Saudi Arabia will continue its hedging policies, maintaining its OPEC+ agreement with Russia over oil quotas and deepening its trading ties to China, perhaps discounting its oil sales, and even pursuing an oil-for-yuan trade, though this objective would remain elusive as long as the Saudi riyal is pegged to the dollar. Over time, the Saudis would likely buy more arms and technology from China and Russia and less from the United States. At a time of intense geopolitical competition, Saudi Arabia's gravitation to a Russo-Chinese alliance would represent a win for them and a strategic setback for the United States.

Unable to rely on the United States for its security but knowing that China and Russia would not sacrifice their relations with Iran for the sake of Saudi security, Saudi Arabia would likely try to find a modus vivendi with Iran. However, it could never afford to rely on Iranian goodwill for its security. Thus, lacking any reliable great power ally to underwrite its security, Saudi Arabia would probably pursue its own nuclear weapons program and shift even more toward Israel, as the two Middle Eastern powers would maintain a common interest in deterring and containing Iran.

For its part, the United States would take a more adversarial approach to Saudi Arabia's decision to hedge with China and side with Russia in keeping oil prices high, as that took a higher toll on Western and developing economies. The Biden administration and Congress would likely adopt an ever more critical view of bin Salman's human rights record and the prosecution of his war in Yemen.

Although this separation between the two countries would be painful, it would also have benefits. If decoupling improves Saudi-Israeli relations, this widening of the "circle of peace" would help stabilize the region. It could also drive a more rational energy policy in the United States or at least compel Washington to seek alternatives to Saudi Arabia's excess oil production capacity to moderate prices, boosting its own shale oil production and encouraging investment in production elsewhere.

Distance would also mitigate the tension at the center of the Biden administration's values-based foreign policy by eliminating the Saudi exception, allowing Biden to narrow the gap between his public pronouncements about his foreign policy and the United States' actual conduct in the world. For their part, the Saudis would be relieved of the burden of a relationship they no longer believe serves their security interests. They could also spend less time and fewer resources fighting an essentially unwinnable battle in Washington over their human rights record and bin Salman's style of rule. The Saudis, like many other leaders in the Middle East, believe the next century belongs to China, and a separation would leave them freer to develop those ties.

This drift toward increasing separation, however, has now been disrupted by the war in Ukraine. With the urgent need to reduce the inflationary effects of high oil prices on Western and developing countries alike, and the equally urgent need to find readily available alternatives to European dependence on Russian oil, the Biden administration is under pressure to abandon the president's rhetoric about placing values at the center of American foreign policy and come to a "realist" understanding with the crown prince. This would involve setting aside the Khashoggi murder and other human rights abuses in an effort to secure bin Salman's commitment to resume Saudi Arabia's traditional role as the swing producer and pump more oil to moderate prices. It might also require an effort to convince Congress to approve new arms sales and extend diplomatic and military support for the Saudis in Yemen should the Houthis continue to resist a political solution to the conflict.

The benefits of such a realist reconciliation are self-evident. For Biden, more oil on the global market means relief at the gas pump for Americans. Relatively inexpensive energy prices are always a winning political issue in the United States. In addition, by dropping objections to the way bin Salman governs, the Biden administration would diminish the Saudi government's desire to expand its ties to Russia and China at the expense of the United States—important in an era of intense great power competition. In turn, the crown prince would no longer need to answer questions about the Khashoggi murder and the treatment of his critics. The pariah would be transformed into a partner again.

Despite the obvious attraction of this approach at a time of crisis for the United States in Europe, none of the fundamental disagreements with Saudi Arabia would be resolved; they would simply be swept under the rug. While Biden could succeed in reaping some political gain from falling prices at the gas pump, congressional criticism would likely grow, particularly (but not exclusively) from the progressive wing of the Democratic Party for whom the abandonment of a values-based policy toward bin Salman would cause outrage. Arms sales, already blocked by Congress, would become unmanageable. The Yemen conflict would continue to rankle.

For his part, bin Salman might enjoy being let out of the penalty box, but that would do nothing to encourage more responsible behavior. The question of American reliability would also remain, and his fundamental security dilemma would soon reassert itself. In time, therefore, with the effects of the war in Ukraine subsiding, the underlying logic of the realist reconciliation would inevitably weaken, rendering it more difficult, if not impossible, to sustain.

A NEW STRATEGIC COMPACT

With separation being undesirable and a realist reconciliation unreliable, then it is timely to consider a more fundamental reconceptualization of the original U.S.-Saudi understanding.

The heart of this new strategic compact would be an agreement to counter the threat from Iran. For the United States, Iran remains the principal source of instability in the Middle East. Its efforts to acquire nuclear weapons, its support for subversive forces across the region, and its hegemonic and sectarian ambitions present a constant challenge to U.S. interests at a time when the United States is preoccupied with greater threats elsewhere. Washington therefore needs reliable and capable regional partners to balance and counter Tehran. As noted earlier, Saudi Arabia can play an important role in that regard.

For Saudi Arabia, Iran, too, represents the principal threat to its interests, particularly the defense of its homeland, the protection of its oil interests, and the internal stability of its wards and friends in the Sunni Arab world. The Saudis worry, however, that the United States prefers to accommodate rather than confront Iran's regional ambitions. They view the original JCPOA as enabling Iran's aggressive policies in the region, and they fear that a return to that deal would have a similar result. Indeed, as Iran nears the nuclear weapons threshold, the Saudis have become focused on how nuclear capabilities could afford Iran protection for even greater regional troublemaking. They are also concerned that a U.S.-Iran rapprochement will empower Iran to fill the vacuum left by a U.S. withdrawal from the region.

This explains why bin Salman raised the idea with Biden administration officials who recently met him of a security guarantee similar to that of the North Atlantic Treaty Organization (NATO), in which an attack on Saudi Arabia would be treated as an attack on the United

States. (The UAE and Egypt have requested similar security guarantees.) Put simply, Saudi Arabia is looking to the United States to provide
a more reliable deterrent against Iran's nuclear and regional ambitions
and more effective means to defend itself against the missile and drone
attacks of Iran's proxies. This indicates that, notwithstanding his pique
at Biden, the crown prince remains interested in a new security understanding with the United States. That opens the door to a more fundamental reimagining of the U.S.-Saudi relationship.

At its foundations, this new compact would require the United
States to recognize the growing importance of Saudi Arabia to American interests in the Middle East, and the consequences that would
flow from that reality. And Saudi Arabia would need to recognize the
responsibilities that would come from assuming a constructive role as a
pillar of stability in a U.S.-supported Middle Eastern order.

On that basis, the two sides would need to negotiate a package of
reciprocal steps in which both sides would make parallel commitments to
each other. The precise contents of this package would require a detailed
negotiation, but the basic elements can be outlined. Given the distrust
that now exists in the relationship, and the difficulty of some of the steps,
it will be necessary to adopt an incremental approach, putting in place the
essential building blocks first and constructing a more elaborate structure
over time as each side demonstrates its commitment and reliability. Nevertheless, it would be important to agree on a road map from the outset.

U.S. SECURITY ASSURANCES

To deal with the reliability gap, the United States would need to be pre-
pared to provide security assurances to Saudi Arabia, which could come

in a variety of forms. A NATO-like treaty commitment to consider an attack on Saudi Arabia as an attack on the United States would require a formal guarantee endorsed by two-thirds of the Senate. Given Saudi Arabia's low standing in Congress, that is simply unachievable even if it were desirable. However, the United States could reemphasize the Carter Doctrine's general pledge to prevent any attempt by a hostile power to gain control of the Gulf region. It could then enter into a Strategic Framework Agreement with Saudi Arabia, as it has done with Singapore, for example. That agreement provides a U.S. commitment to enhance bilateral defense and security cooperation to deal with common threats and promote regional peace and stability.[32] While this combination does not provide a security guarantee, it would commit the United States to maintaining a favorable balance of power in the region and provide the means necessary for Saudi Arabia to defend itself through much closer defense cooperation with the United States. Those verbal commitments could be buttressed by establishing formal consultative mechanisms, joint military exercises, integrated defenses, and other hard-power manifestations of an American commitment to Saudi security.

If a higher degree of reciprocation were justified by Saudi behavior, the United States could also commit to immediate consultations in the event of an urgent security threat to the kingdom and to respond in accordance with its constitutional processes. That would mirror the Australia, New Zealand, and U.S. Security (ANZUS) Treaty (albeit without congressional endorsement) and the consultative procedures outlined in Article 4 of the NATO Treaty.[33] The United States could also borrow from the Taiwan Relations Act and commit to treating an attack on Saudi Arabia as a threat to the peace and security of the Gulf and "of grave concern to the United States." Similarly, President Biden could commit to making available the necessary arms to enable Saudi Arabia to "maintain sufficient self-defense capabilities."[34] That would, of course, require congressional acquiescence, which would be forthcoming only if the Biden administration could point to Saudi actions that justified it.

None of those assurances provide the ironclad commitment of NATO that would automatically treat an attack on Saudi Arabia as an attack on the United States. That would depend on the circumstances. But the more Saudi Arabia acted like a reliable ally, the more the United States would feel obliged to come to the kingdom's defense. And the deeper the defense cooperation and interoperability of defense systems, the more credible the deterrent and the more likely an appropriate military response from the United States.

If the current negotiations to return to the JCPOA nuclear agreement break down and Iran continues its advance to the nuclear threshold, the United States would also need to consider extending a nuclear umbrella to Saudi Arabia in exchange for a Saudi commitment to forgo any acquisition of an independent nuclear capability, including forgoing uranium enrichment. Providing Saudi Arabia with some form of nuclear umbrella would represent a far-reaching commitment by the United States. However, the United States has already committed to preventing Iran from acquiring nuclear weapons. The more that commitment seems in doubt, the more necessary extended deterrence will become. The alternative could well be a Saudi Arabia that seeks its own nuclear weapons, helping to fuel a nuclear arms race in the Middle East.

SAUDI RECIPROCAL STEPS

At a time when Biden is preoccupied with fighting a proxy war with Russia in the heart of Europe and countering a rising China in Asia, and the nation is weary of engaging in wars in the Middle East, a new security commitment to a Gulf ruler who is deeply unpopular on Capitol Hill would be a heavy lift. To make it worthwhile for the Biden administration and marketable to Congress and the American public, bin Salman would need to undertake several reciprocal steps over time that would demonstrate his willingness to play the role of a reliable partner.

First, Saudi Arabia would need to make a more formal open-ended commitment to use its excess oil production to stabilize oil prices at reasonable levels. This move would require it to change its OPEC+ production quota agreement with Russia—or at least not renew it when it expires in September 2022—and boost its oil production to provide Europe with an alternative to dependence on Russian oil exports. Such actions would represent a strategic contribution to the efficacy of sanctions against Russia, immediately improving bin Salman's standing in Washington.

Second, the United States would need to come to an understanding with Saudi Arabia about ending its war in Yemen, if necessary via a unilateral withdrawal. Bin Salman has already shown a willingness to cooperate with his decision in April 2022 to establish a two-month truce with the Houthis. That required Saudi Arabia to agree to partially lift its blockade of the port of Hodeidah and the airport in Sanaa to facilitate the movement of people and goods. Bin Salman also replaced the leadership of the Yemeni government with a presidential council that could further a political process for sharing power in Sanaa. He has provided additional humanitarian aid and financial support for Yemen's banking system. Unfortunately, the Houthis have little incentive to cooperate in such a process while they still believe they can make gains on the battlefield, and neither Saudi Arabia nor the United States can do much to change their calculus. Resuming the Saudi bombing campaign will only increase the humanitarian crisis and fuel opposition in the U.S. Congress. Saudi Arabia therefore needs to begin planning and coordinating with the United States for a unilateral withdrawal from Yemen.

This approach will put the onus for continuing the war on the Houthis and help to salvage Saudi Arabia's reputation with the U.S. Congress. It would also provide the justification for Saudi Arabia's acting in self-defense should the Houthis continue attacks on Saudi soil. By unilaterally withdrawing, the Saudis will avoid depending on Iran to deliver the Houthis and therefore prevent it from extracting a price for doing so. A Saudi willingness to end the war this way would provide further grounds for the Biden administration to commit to Saudi Arabia's defense, in particular by providing it with the weapons and technology to counter Houthi missile and drone attacks and deter cross-border operations from Yemen.

Third, in return for a deeper U.S. security commitment, bin Salman would need to take further steps toward normalizing Saudi Arabia's relations with Israel (e.g., overflight rights, direct flights for Israel's Muslim citizens and Palestinian Muslims in the West Bank and Gaza to make the pilgrimage to Mecca, direct telecommunications, Saudi participation with Israel in regional meetings, and opening of trade offices). This would help consolidate the Israeli-Sunni Arab strategic partnership that has found expression in the Abraham Accords and the March 2022 Negev Summit and enhance its effectiveness by legitimizing Israel's military role in the Arab world and facilitating strategic cooperation against the common threat from Iran.

Saudi Arabia's ability to play a leading role in this coalition will be constrained by its limited military capabilities, as manifested in its failed war in Yemen and its inability to defend itself against Houthi and Iranian attacks. By coordinating with more capable, like-minded regional partners, Saudi Arabia could make up for these military inadequacies. The combined military capabilities of Egypt, Israel, Jordan, and the UAE are impressive, and those states already cooperate extensively on security issues, backed by the United States. Saudi Arabia's primary contribution to this burgeoning Arab-Israeli partnership would derive from the influence it wields as one of the world's top two oil producers and as the leader of the Muslim world. In this way, Saudi Arabia could contribute to a U.S.-supported regional security framework capable of effectively countering Iran, its proxies, and other nonstate actors that seek to disrupt the emerging regional order.

Taking meaningful steps toward normalizing relations with Israel would also change the way Saudi Arabia is viewed by many congressional members from both parties who believe promoting Israel's security and well-being serves U.S. interests. It would garner the enthusiastic support of the pro-Israel community, which could provide considerable political backing for whatever U.S. security assurance is agreed upon.

Saudi Arabia's willingness to move beyond its current posture toward Israel, however, will require progress on resolving the Israeli-Palestinian conflict. For Israel, Saudi Arabia is the crown jewel in the normalization process. The United States could use Saudi willingness to take steps that normalize relations to encourage Israel to take reciprocal steps toward the Palestinians, such as freezing settlement activity beyond the barrier and ceding more West Bank territory to Palestinian control, which would help incrementally rebuild trust and provide a basis for eventual final-status negotiations. Saudi overt participation in this effort, alongside Egypt and Jordan, could do much to contribute to the ultimate compromises necessary for resolving the Israeli-Palestinian conflict.

Finally, if Biden is to overcome his revulsion with the human rights abuses committed during bin Salman's de facto rule and welcome him into the Oval Office, the crown prince would have to make clear that he takes responsibility for the Khashoggi murder, will bring all those directly responsible to justice, and will ensure that such travesties are not repeated.[35] He would also need to continue constraining the country's religious establishment, restricting the religious police's prerogatives, granting women equal rights, and promoting a reformist, inclusive, and tolerant image of Islam internationally.

CONCLUSION

With the United States now focused on a proxy war with Russia in Ukraine and a rising China in Asia, Biden and bin Salman could take the easy way out and continue on their separate ways, coping with high oil prices on the one side and an increasingly dangerous neighborhood on the other without relying on each other. Or they could return to the realist compact that worked well for the first five decades of U.S.-Saudi relations, even though that approach is not sustainable over time and the costs for U.S. interests, should it fail again, could become considerable. In either case, outside powers would seek to fill the vacuum left by the United States in the Gulf, Iran would increase its efforts to assert its hegemony over the Arab world, and a nuclear arms race could take off in the volatile Middle East. Saudi Arabia, too, will hardly be more secure if that scenario unfolds. The risks and costs to both sides associated with these two alternatives make it imperative to consider a third way of negotiating a reciprocal process of strategic rapprochement. Such an effort is admittedly a tall order, requiring a mutual commitment and a sustained seriousness of purpose on both sides. At a time when the United States is preoccupied elsewhere, taking on a new security commitment in the Middle East looks like a repudiation of the bipartisan effort of the last three presidents to end U.S. engagement in the Middle East's conflicts. Yet, without U.S. support for a more stable Middle Eastern order, the United States will be dragged back into conflicts there sooner than war-weary Americans imagine because events in the Middle East directly affect American security interests. Moreover, the crisis in Ukraine and Iran's advancing nuclear program have together created a plastic moment in which major adjustments to the U.S.-Saudi relationship become possible to contemplate and necessary to achieve, especially given potential immediate benefits, such as opening the Saudi oil spigot and relieving the pressure in the oil market.

Saudi Arabia, too, would have to make difficult sacrifices to achieve the new compact, breaking—or at least not renewing—its quota agreement with Russia and moving back into the American orbit with all that would mean for its current policies at home and abroad.

Nevertheless, to manage the multiple crises of this era in the Middle East and beyond, the United States needs a responsible Saudi partner, and Saudi Arabia needs a reliable U.S. one. Seventy-seven years after President Roosevelt met King Abdulaziz, the time has come for the United States and Saudi Arabia to secure the future of their relationship by attempting to achieve a new strategic compact for the twenty-first century.

ENDNOTES

1. Bruce Riedel, *Kings and Presidents: Saudi Arabia and the United States Since FDR* (Washington, DC: Brookings Institution Press, 2018).

2. In an interview with the *Atlantic* published at the same time, the Saudi crown prince said that he didn't care whether Biden understood him because alienating Saudi Arabia would hurt the United States. See Graeme Wood, "Absolute Power," *Atlantic,* March 3, 2022, http://theatlantic.com/magazine/archive/2022/04/mohammed-bin-salman-saudi -arabia-palace-interview/622822.

3. Yaroslav Trofimov, *The Siege of Mecca: The Forgotten Uprising in Islam's Holiest Shrine and the Birth of Al Qaeda* (New York: Doubleday, 2007).

4. Kim Ghattas, *Black Wave: Saudi Arabia, Iran and the Forty-Year Rivalry That Unraveled Culture, Religion and Collective Memory in the Middle East* (New York: Henry Holt, 2020).

5. Hal Brands, Steven A. Cook, and Kenneth M. Pollack, "Why America Shouldn't Abandon the Middle East," *Foreign Policy* (Spring 2020), 50–57.

6. Hal Brands, *Making the Unipolar Moment: U.S. Foreign Policy and the Rise of the Post– Cold War Order* (Ithaca, NY: Cornell University Press, 2016): 239.

7. President Harry S. Truman's recognition of Israel in 1948 was, from the perspective of King Abdulaziz, a betrayal after President Franklin D. Roosevelt had assured the Saudi monarch that the United States would make no decision on Palestine that would harm the Arab population.

8. At the end of his life in 2015, King Abdullah summoned President Bill Clinton to Riyadh to tell him that he regretted not doing more in December 2000 to convince Yasser Arafat to accept the Clinton Parameters for settling the Israeli-Palestinian conflict.

9. Martin S. Indyk, "Challenges to U.S. Interests in the Middle East: Obstacles and Opportunities" (keynote address to the Washington Institute for Near East Policy, Washington, DC, May 18, 1993).

10. "Country Ratings," Gallup, http://news.gallup.com/poll/1624/perceptions-foreign -countries.aspx.

11. Frank Newport and Igor Himelfarb, "Egypt's Favorable Rating in U.S. Slips to Two-Decade Low," *Gallup,* March 15, 2013, http://news.gallup.com/poll/161372/egypt-favorable-rating-slips-two-decade-low.aspx.

12. Condoleezza Rice, "Remarks at the American University in Cairo," U.S. Department of State Archive, June 20, 2005, http://2001-2009.state.gov/secretary/rm/2005/48328.htm.

13. Jeffrey Goldberg, "The Obama Doctrine," *Atlantic,* April 2016, http://theatlantic.com/magazine/archive/2016/04/the-obama-doctrine/471525.

14. Christopher J. Le Mon, "Moving From Partisan to Peacemaker in Yemen," in *Re-engaging the Middle East: A New Vision for U.S. Policy,* ed. Dafna H. Rand and Andrew P. Miller (Washington, DC: Brookings Institution Press, 2020), 51–53.

15. "Saudi Arabia 'Not Consulted' Over US Strike to Kill Iran General," VOA, January 5, 2020, http://voanews.com/middle-east/voa-news-iran/saudi-arabia-not-consulted-over-us-strike-kill-iran-general; and Yasmine Farouk, "What Does the U.S. Killing of Soleimani Mean for Saudi Arabia?" Carnegie Endowment for International Peace Commentary, January 7, 2020, http://carnegieendowment.org/2020/01/07/what-does-u.s.-killing-of-soleimani-mean-for-saudi-arabia-pub-80722%20.

16. "U.S. Imports by Country of Origin," U.S. Energy Information Administration, http://eia.gov/dnav/pet/PET_MOVE_IMPCUS_A2_NUS_EPC0_IM0_MBBL_A.htm; Daniel Yergin, "America Takes Pole Position on Oil and Gas," *Wall Street Journal,* February 16, 2022.

17. By 2020, only 34 percent of Americans had a favorable view of Saudi Arabia, compared to 65 percent who held an unfavorable view. See "Country Ratings," Gallup, http://news.gallup.com/poll/1624/perceptions-foreign-countries.aspx.

18. Gordon Lubold, Nancy A. Youssef, and Michael R. Gordon, "U.S. Military to Withdraw Hundreds of Troops, Aircraft, Antimissile Batteries from Middle East," *Wall Street Journal,* June 18, 2021, http:// wsj.com/articles/u-s-military-to-withdraw-hundreds-of-troops-aircraft-antimissile-batteries-from-middle-east-11624045575.

19. In 2021, OPEC oil made up only 13 percent of all U.S. crude oil imports, 6 percent of which was from Saudi Arabia. Only 5 percent of total U.S. petroleum imports

came from Saudi sources. See "Oil and Petroleum Products Explained," U.S. Energy Information Administration, April 13, 2021, http://eia.gov/energyexplained/oil-and -petroleum-products/imports-and-exports.php, "Frequently Asked Questions (FAQS), U.S. Energy Information Administration, http://eia.gov/tools/faqs/faq.php?id=709&t=6 and "Saudi Arabia Facts and Figures," Organization of the Petroleum Exporting Countries, http://opec.org/opec_web/en/about_us/169.htm.

20. "Climate Change and International Responses Increasing Challenges to U.S. National Security Through 2040," *National Intelligence Council,* http:// dni.gov/files/ODNI /documents/assessments/NIE_Climate_Change_and_National_Security.pdf.

21. "Saudi Arabia Could Invest $50 billion This Year to Boost Oil Capacity," *Reuters,* March 21, 2022, http:// cnn.com/2022/03/21/energy/saudi-aramco-investment/index.html.

22. Meghan L. O'Sullivan and Jason Bordoff, "Russia Isn't a Dead Petrostate, and Putin Isn't Going Anywhere," *New York Times,* January 27, 2022, http://nytimes.com/2022/01 /27/opinion/ukraine-russia-europe-gas.html?smid=tw-share.

23. "Muhammad bin Salman's Risky Bet in Saudi Arabia," *Economist,* April 24, 2021, http:// economist.com/middle-east-and-africa/2021/04/22/muhammad-bin-salmans-risky -bet-in-saudi-arabia.

24. The attendance of Egypt's foreign minister at the "Negev Summit" in Israel of the Abraham Accords countries in March 2022 signaled a willingness to join the anti-Iran pro-normalization camp. Previously, in 2019, Cairo had resisted Trump administration efforts to join the anti-Iranian Middle East Strategic Alliance.

25. Michael Singh, "Axis of Abraham," *Foreign Affairs,* February 22, 2022, http:// foreignaffairs.com/articles/middle-east/2022-02-22/axis-abraham.

26. "Saudi Crown Prince Offered Abbas $10bn to Accept Trump's Deal, Says Report," *Middle East Eye,* May 1, 2019.

27. Trump and Israeli Prime Minister Benjamin Netanyahu had to make do with a clandestine meeting of bin Salman, Netanyahu, and Secretary of State Mike Pompeo in Neom in November 2020, which was promptly leaked to the Israeli media and denied by the Saudi foreign minister. "Netanyahu, Mossad Chief Fly to Saudi, Hold First Known Meet with Crown Prince," *The Times of Israel,* November 23, 2020.

28. Indiscriminate bombing by Saudi aircraft and the blockading of Yemeni ports have contributed to an estimated death toll of almost a quarter of a million people, half of them from such indirect causes as hunger, disease, and damaged infrastructure. See "UN Humanitarian Office Puts Yemen War Dead at 233,000, Mostly From 'Indirect Causes,'" UN News, December 1, 2020, http://news.un.org/en/story/2020/12/1078972.

29. The UN-negotiated truce that took hold in April 2022 is a case in point. The Saudis were instrumental by removing the interim Yemeni president, allowing oil to flow to Houthi-controlled territory through the port of Hodeidah and people to leave Sanaa on direct flights to Amman and Cairo, providing financial support to stabilize the economy, and putting up $300 million for humanitarian relief. The Houthis agreed, in return, to a two-month, self-policed military freeze. A comprehensive ceasefire and political solution seem far off. See Peter Salisbury, "Behind the Yemen Truce," *International Crisis Group,* April 8, 2022, http://crisisgroup.org/middle-east-north

-africa/gulf-and-arabian-peninsula/yemen/behind-yemen-truce-and-presidential
-council-announcements.

30. Ben Hubbard, Farnaz Fassihi, and Jane Arraf, "Fierce Foes, Iran and Saudi Arabia Secretly Explore Defusing Tensions," *New York Times*, May 1, 2021, http://middleeasteye .net/news/saudi-crown-prince-offered-abbas-10bn-accept-trumps-deal-says-report.

31. Graeme Wood, "Absolute Power," *Atlantic*, March 3, 2022, http://theatlantic.com /magazine/archive/2022/04/mohammed-bin-salman-saudi-arabia-palace-interview /622822.

32. "Strategic Framework Agreement for a Closer Cooperation Partnership in Defense and Security," *U.S. Department of State*, July 12, 2005, https://www.state.gov/05-712.

33. "Australia's Defence Relations with the United States: Appendix B—The ANZUS Treaty," *Parliament of Australia*, April 29, 1952, https://www.aph.gov.au/Parliamentary _Business/Committees/Joint/Completed_Inquiries/jfadt/usrelations/appendixb.

34. "H.R.2479—Taiwan Relations Act," *Congress.Gov*, April 10, 1979, https://www .congress.gov/bill/96th-congress/house-bill/2479/actions.

35. Norah O'Donnell, "Mohammed bin Salman Denies Ordering Khashoggi Murder, but Says He Takes Responsibility for It," *60 Minutes*, September 19, 2019, http://www .cbsnews.com/news/mohammad-bin-salman-denies-ordering-khashoggi-murder-but -says-he-takes-responsibility-for-it-60-minutes-2019-09-29.

ABOUT THE AUTHORS

Steven A. Cook is the Eni Enrico Mattei senior fellow for Middle East and Africa studies and director of the International Affairs Fellowship for Tenured International Relations Scholars at the Council on Foreign Relations (CFR). He is a columnist at *Foreign Policy* magazine and an expert on Arab and Turkish politics, as well as U.S.–Middle East policy. Prior to joining CFR, Cook was a research fellow at the Brookings Institution (2001–02) and a Soref research fellow at the Washington Institute for Near East Policy (1995–96). Cook is the author of *False Dawn: Protest, Democracy, and Violence in the New Middle East*; *The Struggle for Egypt: From Nasser to Tahrir Square*, which won the 2012 gold medal from the Washington Institute for Near East Policy; *Ruling but Not Governing: The Military and Political Development in Egypt, Algeria, and Turkey*; and the forthcoming book *The End of Ambition: America's Past, Present, and Future in the Middle East*. He has also published widely in international affairs journals, opinion magazines, and newspapers and is a frequent commentator on radio and television. Cook holds a BA in international studies from Vassar College, an MA in international relations from Johns Hopkins University's School of Advanced International Studies, and an MA and a PhD in political science from the University of Pennsylvania.

Martin S. Indyk is a distinguished fellow at the Council on Foreign Relations. Indyk served as the U.S. special envoy for the Israeli-Palestinian negotiations from July 2013 to June 2014. Prior to that, he was vice president and director of the Brookings Institution's foreign policy program and a senior fellow and founding director of its Center for Middle East Policy. Indyk served as U.S. ambassador to Israel from 1995 to 1997 and again from 2000 to 2001. He also served as special assistant to Clinton, as senior director for Near East and South Asian affairs at the National Security Council (1993–95), and as assistant secretary of state for Near Eastern affairs in the U.S. Department of State (1997–2000). Before entering government, Indyk was founding executive director of the Washington Institute for Near East Policy for eight years. He is the author of *Innocent Abroad: An Intimate Account of American Peace Diplomacy in the Middle East* and the coauthor of *Bending History: Barack Obama's Foreign Policy* with Michael O'Hanlon and Kenneth Lieberthal. His latest book is *Master of the Game: Henry Kissinger and the Art of Middle East Diplomacy*. Indyk received a bachelor's degree in economics from the University of Sydney and a doctorate in international relations from the Australian National University.

ADVISORY COMMITTEE
The Case for a New U.S.-Saudi Strategic Compact

This report reflects the judgments and recommendations of the authors. It does not necessarily represent the views of members of the advisory committee, whose involvement should in no way be interpreted as an endorsement of the report by either themselves or the organizations with which they are affiliated.

Robert W. Jordan
Southern Methodist University

Brian M. Katulis
Center for American Progress

Prem G. Kumar
Albright Stonebridge Group

Ellen Laipson
George Mason University

Sarah Margon
Open Society Foundations

Jami Miscik
Kissinger Associates, Inc.

Richard W. Murphy
Middle East Institute

Meghan L. O'Sullivan
Harvard Kennedy School

Kenneth Michael Pollack
American Enterprise Institute

Carla Anne Robbins
Council on Foreign Relations

Norman Thomas Roule
Pharos Strategic Consulting LLC

Robert B. Satloff
*The Washington Institute
for Near East Policy*

Gary G. Sick
Columbia University

Amy Davidson Sorkin
New Yorker

James B. Steinberg
*Maxwell School
of Syracuse University*

Frances Fragos Townsend
Activision Blizzard

David G. Victor
University of California, San Diego

Enzo Viscusi
Eni

Joseph L. Votel
Middle East Institute

Mona Yacoubian
United States Institute of Peace

Karen E. Young
Middle East Institute